Luke's Go-cart

Story by Jenny Giles
Illustrations by Rachel Tonkin

Luke and Andrew listened carefully as Miss Bell talked to the class about motors and engines.

"Most of the machines that we use around our homes have a motor that makes them work," she said, "and we're going to list some of them."

Kylie put her hand up.
"Our washing machine has a motor," she said.

"And so has our refrigerator," said Zoe.

"We have a motor in our lawn mower," said Megan.

Luke smiled.
"We just got a new lawn mower," he said, "and my dad has made our old one into a go-cart for me."

3

Everyone turned to look at Luke.

"Have you really got your own go-cart?" asked Megan. "With a **motor** in it?"

"Can you drive it, Luke?" asked Kylie.

"Yes," said Luke. "It doesn't go very fast, but I can drive it around the backyard. My dad holds onto it with a long rope."

"It's a great go-cart," said Andrew.
"His dad pulls a cord to make the motor start. I had a ride on it."

"Oh, I'd love to have a ride!" said Megan.

"So would I!" said Zoe and Kylie together.

"Yes, Luke," said the children.
"Can we see your go-cart?"

"I have an idea," said Miss Bell.
"As you know, our School Fair
is being held this Saturday.
Luke, do you think your father
would bring the go-cart to the fair?
Then we could see how the motor works,
and some of the children
might be able to have a ride."

"I'll ask my dad tonight," said Luke.

When Luke and Andrew arrived at school
the next morning, they ran to see Miss Bell.
"Dad says he'll bring my go-cart
to the School Fair," said Luke.
"He'll bring a helmet and a rope, too,
so that everyone can have a ride."

"Hurray!" shouted the children.

"That's good," said Miss Bell.
"I'll talk to your mom and dad about it later."

On Saturday morning, the children lined up
to have a ride on the go-cart.
Luke's dad showed them
how the steering wheel
turned the front wheels. He told them
that the accelerator made the go-cart
go faster, and that the brake pedal
made the wheels stop.

Then he showed everyone
how he started the motor.
He gripped the end of the cord
and pulled hard.
His arm shot up,
and the motor whirred.

But it didn't start.

Luke's dad pulled the cord again.
Whirr... went the motor.
He pulled the cord again... and again...
Whirr... whirr... went the motor.
And then it was silent.

Go-cart RIDES

Luke was embarrassed.
"What's wrong with it?" he asked.

"I don't think it wants to start,"
said his dad.

"But everyone wants to have a ride!"
cried Luke.

"Well, I'm sorry," replied his dad,
"but they'll just have to sit in it."

So, one by one,
the children sat in the go-cart.
They moved it along with their feet,
and turned the steering wheel.
"It's a good go-cart, Luke," said Megan.
"I like it."

"It's no fun, though,"
said one of the other children.
"The motor doesn't work.
Let's go and do something else."

Everyone wandered away
to other parts of the fair.

"Dad," said Luke,
"can we try it just one more time?"

"I don't think it's going to start today," said Dad. "I'll take it home and have a good look at it."

"**Please**, Dad," begged Luke. "Just **try** it."

Luke's dad bent down over the go-cart.
He gave the cord a strong, sharp pull.
Putt, putt, putt, went the motor.
Putt, putt, putt.
And then it roared into life!

Luke jumped into the go-cart,
and started to drive it.
The children turned around when they heard
the noise of the motor. They ran back
across the playground, shouting and cheering.

Everyone watched the go-cart chugging along.
"Look! The motor **does** work!"
grinned Luke,
as he stopped by the line of children.
"Now, who wants to have a ride
in my go-cart?"